T0198841

Sheryl the Shrink, says...

People Heal When the Talk is Real!

Sheryl Schembari, LCSW

authorHOUSE®

AuthorHouse™
1663 Liberty Drive
Bloomington, IN 47403
www.authorhouse.com
Phone: 1-800-839-8640

Published by AuthorHouse   2/17/2015

ISBN: 978-1-4969-5970-6 (sc)
ISBN: 978-1-4969-5971-3 (hc)
ISBN: 978-1-4969-5969-0 (e)

Library of Congress Control Number: 2014922495

Print information available on the last page.

Any people depicted in stock imagery provided by Thinkstock are models, and such images are being used for illustrative purposes only. Certain stock imagery © Thinkstock.

This book is printed on acid-free paper.

Because of the dynamic nature of the Internet, any web addresses or links contained in this book may have changed since publication and may no longer be valid. The views expressed in this work are solely those of the author and do not necessarily reflect the views of the publisher, and the publisher hereby disclaims any responsibility for them.

Credits

Produced by:

Lions Vision Productions, LLC

Edited by:

LaTia McNeely-Sandiford, MSW

Cover design by:

LaTia McNeely-Sandiford, MSW

Chapter Photographs by:

Marco Schembari

Author Cover & Bio Photos by:

Glamour Shots Studio

National Hotline Numbers by:

Psych Central. (2007). Common Hotline Phone Numbers. *Psych Central*. Retrieved on December 24, 2014, from http://psychcentral.com/lib/common-hotline-phone-numbers/0001302

Dedication

In Life

I dedicate this book to my mother and mentor who provided me with unconditional love and gave me the freedom to express my feelings. The foundation that she established enabled me to be true to myself, empathetic toward others and compassionate towards animals. These traits have helped me immeasurably in my personal and professional lives.

To my father who did the best that he could with what he knew. He gave me what he had to give me and for that, I'm thankful. I know now, both intellectually and emotionally, that he has always loved me. Moreover, I am now aware of the fact that he has perpetually been proud of me.

To my husband, Marco, who has remained in my corner for fourteen years providing love and support. He is my biggest cheerleader and the one who really 'gets' me. Even when I'm too much to handle, he continues to show me devotion and patience.

To my beautiful cat, Lester, who is truly a special soul... always loving, always gentle, and always in my lap purring, making the writing process all the more enjoyable.

And Last But Not Least

To my clients who have helped me more than they know. I'm privileged that they've allowed me to play a part in their journey; without it, this book could never have been written.

In Death

In loving memory of my grandparents, Freida and Max Epstein, who showered me with love, always. They wanted the best for me, but most of all, they made me want the best for me.

Finally, in loving memory of my beloved pets: Marshmallow, Oliver, Cookie, Cody, and Stanley -- rest in peace. All have taught me how to truly love unconditionally and have helped me to become a better person. For that, I am eternally grateful.

Foreword

Sheryl the Shrink, says, is a collection of keenly penetrating analytic observations about life, relationships, and feelings management. The book offers the reader much food for thought on how to make "emotional sense" of intrapsychic and interpersonal conundrums. As a therapist, with over 30 years in the field, I have rarely come upon a book that spans the changes of emotional life, yet, presents in a very clear and pragmatic manner. It will be the unusual reader of this book who does not have that light bulb or "aha" experience, where the written word resonates with the reader's internal perceptions of life.

Most readers will have the response that many clients have in clinical settings of: "That's exactly how I feel", or "Now I understand. It all makes sense". Further, it is always a comfort to know that others "get" our experiences and connect with our life's journey. Perhaps, upon completion of the book, readers might be encouraged to seek further counseling or conduct a deeper self-assessment that will help them to achieve full life satisfaction.

In summary, Sheryl touches on most manners of human emotions and life reflection with humor, examples and clarity that is meant to reach the reader's core. Sheryl is a seasoned, insightful therapist who has a wonderful gift of communication that is very informative, interesting and fun. I highly recommend this book.

Eileen Gutstein, LCSW

Table of Contents

Introduction

Sheryl the Shrink, says, is a compilation of insights, life lessons, observations and strategies by psychotherapist, Sheryl Schembari, LCSW. Sheryl provides practical solutions to common issues that often create barriers in people's lives. According to Sheryl, "The pearls of wisdom contained in this book have helped me, family members, friends, and clients to live according to our authentic selves."

Emotional freedom is a blessing that most of us have trouble experiencing. It allows us the safety to live within our truth. However, in order for people to experience emotional freedom, they must first face the truth about themselves. Psychotherapy helps people access suppressed emotions that enable them to heal and grow. As you read this book, be in your truth, accept your truth and allow yourself the freedom to let go.

The purpose of this book is to give those searching for answers to ordinary problems a tool to achieve immediate success. Each chapter is designed to educate, inspire and empower others to make the best choices that support their emotional freedom.

Note to the Reader

I understand the complexities of embarking on one's own journey of self-help. Many of us spend our entire lives looking outside for answers that often lie within. I encourage you to read this book with an open mind, honest heart and accepting spirit. It provides insight, from one person to another, regarding common issues that tend to reoccur with all of us.

Make this book your diary. It's formatted for you to have the freedom to write all over it. As you read, document your thoughts, feelings, "aha" moments and changes that you wish to make. My prayer for you is that you will digest the information, make any necessary adjustments and learn from my experiences.

Chapter 1 ~ Self-Care

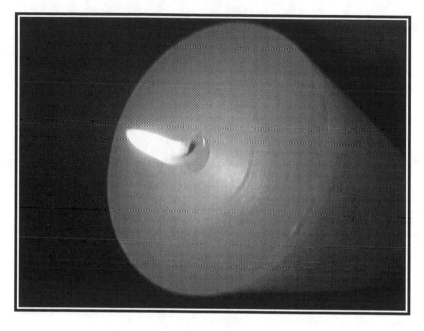

Images available as paintings at

www.sheryltheshrink.com

Sheryl the Shrink, says, "Women listen up: Taking care of yourself and putting yourself first isn't selfish! We are great at taking care of others, but we are the worst at self-care. We women allow ourselves to be depleted by the needs of others because that's what we're trained to do."

What I've Learned - The more you give to yourself, the more you will have to give to others. The practice of "self-care" allows women the space to leave something for themselves and address their own personal needs. Self-care happens when we are unapologetically doing what empowers us and makes us feel better about ourselves. When we practice self-care, we are fully replenished with the energy necessary to keep us going.

In my business, I watch women deplete themselves every day. My office is filled with women on the verge of breakdowns because they've failed to practice self-care. Women enter my practice totally empty, in need of being rebuilt from the inside out. Many times, they've neglected their own physical, mental and emotional health and are left with nothing to give.

Take Away - Take care of you! You are worthy to be number one and you shouldn't have to bottom out before you understand and practice self-care. Take a day for yourself, at least once a week, doing what you love, going where you're most happy and being at peace with you.

Sheryl the Shrink, says, "Play is a mandatory part of adult life. It's easy to get bogged down by the day-to-day activities of adulthood. The monotony of being a 'responsible' adult gets boring. It is imperative to make time to be silly on a regular basis, to be more child-like. Have some fun! Live a little!"

What I've Learned – Adulthood can suck the fun out of life and relationships. When we forget to laugh and have a good time, life becomes too serious. In a world where wars are among us, people are homeless and starving, and any flip of the nightly news shows a society in crisis, we must find the lighter side.

Take Away – Don't be a kill joy! Take time to smell the roses, walk on the sand, roll in the grass and feel the breeze of the ocean. Worrying about this or that does not prove helpful for anyone. Instead, take time doing things that you love and make you feel better as a person.

Sheryl the Shrink, says, "Don't ever make one person your entire world. Be careful of placing your hopes, dreams and aspirations into another person. Women are the greatest offenders of making men our whole universe. This never works for our benefit. Instead, we end up hurt and unfulfilled because we depended on one person to do for us what we should have been doing for ourselves. No one person can make you complete; instead, we must strive for completion within ourselves."

What I've Learned – When we allow ourselves to be validated through the existence of others, we strip ourselves of independent happiness. As a result, absent that other person, we have a difficult time identifying and understanding our own value. This happens a lot with married couples whose spouses predecease them. The wives have very difficult transitions as widows and experience little happiness without their husbands. In older people, many times, the surviving spouse passes shortly after. These deaths are usually preceded by loneliness that led to broken hearts.

Take Away – Enjoy a full life of diversified relationships. In particular, be mindful of nurturing your friendships;

otherwise, they will die. Learn to appreciate the uniqueness that each person in your life brings. Take the time to connect with people through what you have in common and how you may be different.

Sheryl the Shrink, says, "Enjoy quality time alone and powered down. We learn a lot about ourselves when we truly take time to get to know us. We are living in a technological society where we are always plugged in all of the time. The need to be attached to our mobile devices has stripped us of the alone time necessary to decompress."

What I've Learned – Human beings can't operate optimally if they never shut down. People are always in a hurry to go nowhere. Giving yourself five minutes a day to breathe helps clear your mind and de-stress your body. People are more anxious, lethargic and on edge when they don't take time to wind down. Adapting a habit of taking five minutes a day to take deep breaths will not only help you center, but will also allow you to think clearly. What good is being alive if we never take the time to live?

Take Away – You can't be enjoyable to someone else, if you can't stand to be alone with you. Take the time to be in your own space so that you can better love and accept yourself. Alone time gives us reflection space that helps us to see things more lucidly. When you take time to be alone, you gain greater understanding and clarity. Enjoy alone time, often.

Sheryl the Shrink, says, "Do not spend your entire life distracting yourself from yourself in order to avoid feeling some sort of emotional pain or discomfort."

What I've Learned - Most people numb themselves in a myriad of ways, e.g., watching television for hours on end, overeating, shopping, gambling, engaging in substance abuse and/or overworking, just to avoid feeling something uncomfortable. People who feel the need to constantly be engaged are in an intentionally perpetual state of distraction. Why?

Take Away – Self-assessment is a necessary form of self-care. Many of us spend so much time running from ourselves that we never get to know who we are. Who are you? Why are you? Where are you going? Why? How are you going to get there? These are the questions left unanswered when we are eternally engaged in a flutter of activities designed to distract us from these matters.

Chapter 2 ~ Emotions

Images available as paintings at

www.sheryltheshrink.com

Sheryl the Shrink, says, "People often repeat the same dysfunctional patterns because they are subconsciously looking for a corrective emotional experience."

What I've Learned - Men and women seek in their partners what they've been accustomed to know of the other gender from their opposite sex parent. For example, a really nice man could be stuck in a vicious cycle of forever dating bitches because his mother, who was his first powerful role model of the opposite sex, is a bitch. Therefore, he will spend the rest of his life in tumultuous relationships with bitches because those are the characteristics that he associates with women. Without the tools to rectify the behaviors with his mother, he becomes trapped in a pathology that he repeats (and will more than likely pass on to his children).

Take Away – Tell people how they make you feel. Instead of displaying masked emotions, tell others how what they say and do directly impacts you. If you practice this communication strategy, then you'll reap the rewards by means of healthy relationships. While we can't change people, we can change how we allow them to treat us.

Sheryl the Shrink, says, "We all need to feel connected. It is priceless when others accept the essence of who we are as people. We all thrive best in relationships where there's freedom to be ourselves without judgment.

This sense of being is pivotal to forming associations that allow bonds to form."

What I've Learned – Emotional connections are the epicenter of relationships. People thrive best in environments where they feel safe to be themselves and share their emotions. Whether your connection is based on mutual interest, culture, or anything else, you are empowered by the ability to share your innermost thoughts in a nonjudgmental environment. For this reason, people flock to my office. Many times, individuals are simply seeking a safe place to dispel their emotions.

Take Away – Take the time to be present. When you are emotionally present, it allows for greater opportunities to relate with people on a deeper level. It is through that process, or connection, that people build trust that develops the foundation for healthy relationships.

Sheryl the Shrink, says, "The hallmark of emotional maturity is the ability to persevere in spite of how you feel. Unlike children who demand immediate gratification, adults are expected to work through their feelings for the greater good or to complete a specific project. While the ability to work through emotions is ideal, many adults are unsuccessful because they aren't equipped with the necessary skills to do so."

What I've Learned – As a mega multitasker (and occasional procrastinator), I sometimes allow the 'busy' of everyday life to get in the way of my basic household chores. Depending on how I'm feeling, I have a habit of waiting until the last minute to get things done. However, what I've learned about myself is that the 'chaos', that is sometimes my laundry room, is often reflective of my emotional state at the time. If I'm overwhelmed with emotion (as we women are at that time of the month), I'm less likely to make my household duties a priority. For me, this process doesn't end until I begin to think about the impact of my actions on the ones I love. Then, wife guilt kicks in and despite how I feel, I get the laundry done. I know my husband depends on me for fresh clean clothes, so his needs become primary.

Take Away – Learn to identify your emotions. Do your best to check in on your emotions and experience the reasons for why you feel a particular way. Observe your surroundings, time of the month, people in your space and times of the day, week or year. Do you recognize any patterns? What are your triggers? If you recognized patterns, it's important to get to the root. For most of us, it takes a professional to guide us through this process. If you need help, do so because your emotional stability depends on it (so does the well-being of others).

Sheryl the Shrink, says, "People are in control of you when they can control your emotions. Some people get a thrill out of pissing others off, just to get a reaction. When you allow those people the satisfaction of a response, they have exerted power over you. Your negative response then strips you of your emotional, physical and spiritual growth. Learn to be the bigger person."

What I've Learned - Whenever I find myself having an exaggerated, over-the-top reaction to something minor, I try to check in on that emotion (yes, I said, 'try', I'm a therapist, I'm human). As with most of us, the immediate issue is rarely the root of my response. More often than not, I'm reacting to a past event that the current event triggered in my mind. For instance, I'm ultra-sensitive to situations where I feel as if I'm not being acknowledged. This shortcoming is undoubtedly a residual of feeling emotionally abandoned by my father growing up. My disproportionate response often cues my husband to prompt me. Then, once prompted, I'm immediately forced to weigh in on what I'm feeling in my heart and why.

Take Away - If you catch yourself having a strong emotional response to something, stop and ask yourself, "Is my reaction appropriate to the incident? Am I responding to this situation or a prior situation?" Try to take a self-control strategy, count to ten, and take time to de-escalate. Usually, an immediate self-control technique gives us the minute needed to decrease the intensity of our reactions. This will benefit all parties involved. The ability to use a self-control method during times of frustration decreases the likelihood that you'll have to make an apology later.

Sheryl the Shrink, says, "Sarcasm is either the lowest form of humor or a socially acceptable form of anger. From my experience, people who exhibit chronic sarcasm are venting their aggressive feelings in an indirect way that does not defy social norms. Sarcastic people use passive aggressive ways to both deliver obvious messages and vent their hostility. Though it is often meant humorously and intended as a joke, and sometimes is genuinely funny, sarcasm usually relies on putting another person down or making someone else feel small."

What I've Learned – Through my work with people and study of human behavior, I've learned that there are several reasons that someone might be sarcastic. The question you have to ask yourself is, "Is this passive sarcasm designed to be humorous with an unintentional impact of upsetting you? Or is it aggressive sarcasm that is designed to be intentionally belittling and/or hurtful?"

Take Away – Sarcasm is another form of communication. Sometimes its effectiveness brings home an obvious point, but other times it's used to make others feel insignificant. Be careful of sarcastic delivery, for you never know how the person listening will take your comment.

Chapter 3 ~ Baggage

Images available as paintings at

www.sheryltheshrink.com

Sheryl the Shrink, says, "There is a purpose to your pathology, or reasons for the ailments in your life. Much of our pain derives from unresolved issues from our childhood. More often than not, the root of our issues (and we all have them), starts early in our lives and reinvents itself in our adulthood."

What I've Learned - I have several clients who were not properly nurtured by either parent, having forced them to essentially raise themselves. When people grow up in this manner, it creates abandonment, rejection and attachment issues (amongst others) that lead adults to my office. Many times, it takes years of therapy to get these individuals to process their pain and use it for their purpose.

Take Away - Understand the root of your pain. We must always be on a steady trend of self-assessing. Self-assessment allows us to get deep and honest with ourselves to understand how we play a part in our own mess. As opposed to deflecting our stuff onto unsuspecting individuals (like our kids and spouses), we are then able to see what we need to change.

We all have issues that we have to work through to make us well-rounded adults. Generally, until we work on these issues, we end up repeating patterns of dysfunction. When women are carrying around, *Burdens in their Backpacks* (homage to my friend, author LaTia McNeely-Sandiford), they often have a hard time establishing careers, building healthy relationships, managing their weight and dealing with life in general.

Sheryl the Shrink, says, "Know your truth. It is only through the truth that we gain understanding of who we are, why we are and what we want out of life. When we are truthful with ourselves, it's much easier to be honest with the world."

What I've learned - My husband and I have made the conscious decision not to have children. While we both adore and have an affection to nurture animals, we don't have the passion to be parents. This is our truth. Albeit, not a decision made by most adults, but for us it works and we've allowed ourselves the freedom to live in it – happily.

Take Away - When you try to please everyone else, you end up in misery. The best way to approach life is to live in your truth, not the desires of others. In all that you do, be authentic to you because 'peace' illuminates in truth.

When you are living honestly, you are free to explore life as an open vessel, on your terms.

Sheryl the Shrink, says, "What you are not conscious of controls you. If you are not self-aware and accepting of your own inner feelings, thoughts, beliefs and shortcomings, it will continue to mindlessly happen. Therefore, you run the risk of existing haphazardly. Instead of being aware of what's occurring, you then allow life to happen to you, instead of for you. When we are self-aware, there is little that other people can say or do to control us. Instead, we remain in control of ourselves and thereby operate the driver's seat in our lives."

What I've Learned - Years ago, when I was in counseling, I discovered that I had an unconscious pattern of dating guys who were always unavailable to me in some way. I found myself settling for a partial of what I deserved because for me, a little was better than nothing. In order to break this pathology, I had to accept the truth that no one would be able to fill the void that my father left. Instead, I had to acknowledge and accept the fact that he wasn't emotionally available and release the longing that I transferred through my expectations of men. When I realized what I'd been doing, I was able to change my behavior. Therefore, I began to consciously make concerted efforts to be in relationships with men who were totally available. When I raised my expectations and stopped settling, I took back my own power.

Take Away - Try to uncover the etiology of your emotional baggage through ongoing self-inventory. We are all imperfect; however, we have a duty to be self-aware so that we are more equipped to make conscious choices. As a result, we become empowered and better prepared to control our actions and emotions.

Sheryl the Shrink, says, "Being self-sufficient is a pre-cursor for being in a healthy relationship. People should be involved with a romantic partner out of 'want' not 'need'. A person, who enters a relationship without the means or mindset to meet his/her own basic needs, does so from a subservient place. As the relationship evolves, this person then becomes even less empowered and more unfulfilled."

What I've Learned - People who engage in co-dependent relationships have insecurities that derive from past experiences. For some, it's a lack of marketable skills, but for others it a lack of self-esteem. In this day and time, it's important that both parties have equal footing in the relationship. Equality is best established when each person has the ability, means and freedom to manage his/her own life independent of the other.

Take Away – Have a mindset to create the means to meet your basic needs. Women, especially, should always keep a nest egg and continually seek advancement opportunities to create resources. It's important that you are able to make decisions about your future without the permission of your partner, should that relationship sour. Men, if you are in a position of financial leadership in the relationship, your significant other shouldn't feel less valued. Relationships are partnerships that are best experienced when each person feels equal.

Sheryl the Shrink, says, "Be mindful of when you're being judgmental because you could be digging into your own baggage. We all have a propensity to prejudge things based on our own morals, values, experiences and beliefs. However, we need to be conscious that each of those categories is different for each person. The old adage couldn't be truer, 'You can't judge a book by its cover.'"

What I've Learned – There is no place for judgment in my line of work. If I wasn't able to separate my baggage (and we all have it) from those of my clients, I would be doing them a disservice. People come to me with a host of issues, and my job is to help them process without interjecting my personal thoughts, feelings and experiences. In the profession of Social Work, I've realized that our heightened sense of empathy makes being nonjudgmental easier, but still we're human. The truth is, we all form an opinion at some point. However, I make a concerted effort to meet people where they are and understand that all of our journeys are different.

Take Away – Check your emotional baggage. Be sure you aren't displacing your stuff onto others by judging their experiences, behaviors, feelings or habits. Instead of judging, pray for those with whom you have differences. Ask God to help you to understand their plight while equipping you with tools or words of comfort to show you care.

Chapter 4 ~ Environment

Images available as paintings at

www.sheryltheshrink.com

Sheryl the Shrink, says, "Your physical surroundings affect your mood and can determine how, when, or if you progress. You've heard it said that your home is your sanctuary, well, that's true. For this reason, it is important to make your home aesthetically pleasing to your taste.

Even if you are on a tight budget, try to make your dwelling as calming and cheerful as possible."

What I've Learned – A cluttered home is often reminiscent of a chaotic life. If you want to organize your mind, start by organizing your physical space. Begin with one room at a time to minimize feeling overwhelmed. The pivotal areas are the ones that you frequent often, for example, the kitchen, the living room, and your master bedroom. Anything that takes up space gives off energy that you absorb into your being, so clean up!

I am totally energized by my home. The rooms in my house are brightly colored, organized, and exude wide open space. Whenever I am in these areas, my spirits are automatically uplifted and I feel fully alive.

Take Away – If you want to live a clutter-free life, you should start by uncluttering the thoughts in your mind. Our environments can dictate the messages that resonate in our souls. Manage your environment and create a happier ending in your life.

Sheryl the Shrink, says, "It is very important to be your own person and individualize, especially from your family and environment of origin. Many people unconsciously hold themselves back from fully individualizing because they fear being ostracized and/or isolated. This mentality keeps gay people in the closet and cycles of abuse hidden as family skeletons. In fact, sometimes, based on our surroundings, people must adapt a different image for their own advancement."

What I've Learned – Being true to who you are doesn't mean denouncing where you're from. People can effectively adapt their own morals, values, beliefs and customs, separate from their families (and places) of origin. This is especially necessary when individuals come from dysfunctional families and impoverished environments.

Take Away - Being your own person goes deeper than accepting all of you, (good, bad & ugly); it encompasses accepting the parts of your life that aren't desirable. Sometimes we want to separate ourselves from our adversity, when, in fact, we should embrace it and use it to teach others. Individuals can successfully individualize while holding the elements of themselves that shape them as people. We are molded by our families, environments, society and our own thoughts and feelings.

Sheryl the Shrink, says, "As people, we all thrive in environments that are conducive to our mental, physical, emotional, psychological and spiritual needs. However, in reality, we all derive from some level of dysfunction. So, the question becomes, how do you cope in your dysfunction? Are you someone who internalizes your environment or do you take the best from your environment and allow it to shape you as a person? Well, for individuals who are destined to be successful, the latter is true. For this reason, we must learn coping skills that allow us to live inside our environments, without being consumed by the inner workings and negative distractions of our surroundings."

What I've Learned - People who are determined to be successful are not distracted by what's going on around them. Instead, these people are on an absolute path to achieve the very best that life has to offer. Usually, these people are driven by forces that are greater than their environments. What drives these people vary, but the commonality is that these individuals don't allow outside forces to take them off their game. As we live this thing called life, we must be mindful of minefields that are embedded in our paths to set us off course. Sometimes, these things are sent in the form of people, places and/or things. However, if you have learned the necessary skills to divert pitfalls, then, you are half-way to achieving your goals despite negative influences in your surroundings.

Take Away – Your environment is where you live, where you come from or where you frequent, but it's not who you are. You are one of great strength and purpose who may not feel validated by what you see. However, just know that you are uniquely and wonderfully made with a gift that shines no matter your locale. You are only as stifled as you allow yourself to be.

Sheryl the Shrink, says, "Growing up or raising children in an environment that doesn't provide a realistic world view is very damaging. Due to guilt or insecurities, parents often overcompensate by showering their children with material things. As a result, these children grow up with a sense of entitlement and are emotionally crippled. The real world operates under a different set of rules."

What I've Learned - When children fail to establish a strong work ethic or understand the concept of "earning", they approach life with unrealistic expectations. These patterns or thought processes carry into adulthood and these people develop unhealthy relationships with money. I live in an area where it isn't unheard of for parents to buy their 17 year-old children BMW's as rites of passage. These children have no concept of a dollar and often treat those who aren't on the same financial level as less than worthy. When these children inevitably become adults, they will lack a sense of internal pride that comes from earning stuff on their own instead of things being handed to them.

Take Away – Teach your children the concept of earning for a job well-done. Implement a rewards system that reinforces children for positive behavior and encourages realistic goals and aspirations. The ability for adults to make sound life decisions often begins with whether or not the concept was introduced to them as children. If they are taught at an early age about 'work and reward', they are better equipped to make appropriate life choices about other things.

Sheryl the Shrink, says, "When parents have children at young ages, sometimes a sense of rivalry is created between the same sex parent and child. These feelings can initiate from either the child or the parent. The home environment then becomes competitive in nature, decreasing the likelihood for a nurturing atmosphere to exist."

What I've Learned – In my practice, I have seen this dysfunction play out with both female and male clients. The females had mothers who perceived them as a competitive sister, and the males had fathers who viewed them as a competitive brother. Many times this setting isn't created intentionally; rather, it is created when parents and their children are of the same generation. For this reason, it is important that young parents have support from more mature adults. Sometimes it's necessary for young parents to have help setting boundaries and guidelines that structure the parent/child relationship.

Take Away – Young parents often need additional support from mature adults to increase the probability of establishing an environment that is both healthy and nurturing.

Chapter 5 ~ Relationships

Images available as paintings at

www.sheryltheshrink.com

Sheryl the Shrink, says, "Know when it's time to let go or mend fences. Relationships with women and men can be emotionally draining. However, you are in control of how you allow a relationship to impact you. Much of what you receive in a relationship will depend on how you respond to the other's actions."

What I've learned - People respond to how they're treated. When in doubt about whether you should act a particular way towards someone, ask yourself if any good can come out of your response. If what you are about to say or do does not perform a useful function, then don't do it. Instead, retreat and decide whether the payoff is worth the energy output. This is when we are left the decision to cut ties or mend fences.

Take Away – Always be in a mode of 'self-preservation'. This keeps your needs at the forefront at all times. The fact that relationships can take a toll on us means that we have the responsibility of protecting ourselves from emotional burnout. Think before you act and think harder about the people you are engaging.

We all are responsible for utilizing our personal energy in ways that benefit the relationship. People function best when there is a great level of respect and communication. When those things are in place, and the need to confront a specific topic arises, a thoughtful exchange can occur between two people. However, this is much harder said than done so each party should first complete a self-check. Ask yourself, "Is the output of negative energy worth the reward? Will it ultimately make a difference in the relationship or how someone sees a particular situation?" If not, think twice and strategize another solution.

Sheryl the Shrink, says, "The real tragedy of having a series of failed relationships is the questioning of your own judgment. If you have a pattern of selecting emotionally damaged people, then you have to ask yourself, 'What's wrong with my internal compass? Why do I choose partners who inevitably disappoint me and/or are emotionally unavailable? What is broken in me'?"

What I've Learned – Broken people attract broken people. People who have unresolved issues send signals that are familiar to other people with unresolved issues. It's important that as we go from relationship to relationship, we give ourselves time to reflect. Reflection allows for a 'hindsight' view that enables us to see our situation with fresh eyes. In that process, we are better able to identify the role we've played in the deterioration of the relationship and identify what we need to work on about ourselves.

Take Away – Use the time when you are not in a relationship to work on your shortcomings. Each time we end a relationship, we should be learning new things about ourselves. We all possess certain character flaws that negatively impact our ability to have loving partnerships. However, it is up to us to identify those issues and work on them.

Sheryl the Shrink, says, "When it comes to relationships, the opposite of love is not hate; it's actually apathy. Love and hate are on the same continuum; they both show a strong level of feeling and attachment. Apathy, on the other hand, displays a total lack of feeling and emotional detachment."

What I've Learned - When I see people for couples counseling, I tell them that it's a good sign if they love or even hate each other because there is an intense emotional involvement with one another either way. This gives me hope for healing the relationship. However, when there is apathy, there is no hope for the relationship, as they are emotionally checked out and disconnected from the partnership. A state of apathy doesn't happen overnight. Rather, this is a state that a relationship reaches after long periods of dissatisfaction. At this level, one or both of the partners no longer see the benefit of the union, resentment has grown and hearts have become hardened. Rarely does the relationship have an opportunity to mend after this point. Instead, the couple finds reasons (excuses) to stay, such as children, financial dependency or lack of resources. These reasons then become the sole purpose for continuing the union.

Take Away - If you have doubt as to whether it's the right time to end a relationship, you'll know it's time if you develop a lack of feeling, emotion, interest and concern towards him/her. If you are or identify your partner as being at this point, do everyone a favor and terminate the relationship because nothing good can come out of it. Healthy partnerships are only attainable and sustainable if there is an emotional connection between the two parties involved.

Sheryl the Shrink, says, "There is often a kind of emotional tap dance in relationships where one partner is open and the other person is closed. These types of individuals usually have a difficult time connecting because the open person is willing to reveal, while the closed person is very guarded. Why does this happen? The answer is simple -- fear. People are afraid of being hurt."

What I've Learned – A hardened heart is an unhappy heart. People who have been hurt in relationships never lose the feeling of what it was like to experience that type of rejection. For some, the memories are so traumatic that they swear off love for good. When hurt hearts open themselves up again, they do so with such extreme caution that it's laborious for the other partner to be with them. For this reason, rebounding is a bad idea. When you experience a breakup, you must give yourself time to recoup and reflect.

Take Away - Do not deprive yourself of the possibility of being in love. We've all had broken hearts, but if you close yourself off to romance, you rob yourself of the opportunity to truly experience the beauty of love in reciprocity.

Sheryl the Shrink, says, "Many people remain with their significant others because of attachment, not love. When you are attached to a person, you usually share a long history. Frequently, you've grown so accustomed to him/her that the relationship becomes co-dependent. Then, the thought of being without the partner produces anxiety. Love, on the other hand, comes from a much deeper place of caring and connectedness. It is the feeling of wanting to be with someone because this person enhances your life and truly magnifies your happiness."

What I've Learned – People are creatures of habit. We behave a particular way for such a while that we don't seek other ways to achieve the same goal. In long-term relationships, this is especially true. We stay with people when things aren't right because we fear the unknown. After you've been with someone for a long period of time, he/she becomes almost predictable. For many, the predictability is less risky than not knowing the behaviors of someone new. The older we get, the truer this becomes. When we are in advanced years, we almost are never willing to start over, even after the deaths of our spouses.

Take Away - Love comes from the heart and attachment comes from the head. Be sure that you are listening to the right organ when making decisions about love.

Chapter 6 ~ Dating

Images available as paintings at

www.sheryltheshrink.com

Sheryl the Shrink, says, "You must kiss a lot of frogs before you get to your prince. It's not until you've reached a certain level of maturity before you truly know what you need and want in a man. Therefore, you must allow yourself time to go through this process with the frogs."

What I've Learned – A healthy well-balanced relationship is developed when two people have been with enough people to know what they don't want. Through that process, people learn much about themselves and what they desire in a prospective mate.

In my practice, I've seen countless couples who have been together since high school, sometimes even junior high, and have never experienced companionship from anyone other than their partner. In a sense, they have robbed themselves of the spice of life, that is, variety. Variety helps us to discern the good fruit from the bad fruit. It's through dating an assortment of people that we learn about what we like in relationships and what qualities are really important to us. Having a lot of dating experience helps us to build a prototype of the person with whom we ultimately want to establish a relationship. For the most part, the weaning out process of dating is supposed to prepare us for our spouses.

Take Away – Get out there before you make your final selection. Personally, I am extremely grateful for my years of dating before having met my husband. As a result, I was able to receive my husband and appreciate his qualities. I was mature enough to understand that while he wasn't (still isn't) perfect, his good outweighed his bad. For this reason, I've learned to appreciate him and understand his quirks. When you have this level of understanding, the rough days are more tolerable, which is what it takes to be in love for the long haul.

Sheryl the Shrink, says, "Shut up and listen! One of the greatest skills a person can encompass is being a good listener. The art of listening allows for greater connections, deeper understanding and quality conversations. Someone's ability to listen is an asset that can be used personally and professionally."

What I've Learned – Nobody likes to be around an egocentric person. The need to talk repeatedly, especially about oneself, is the characteristic of a bad listener. Individuals who are self-absorbed have a hard time listening because it requires them to stop talking. However, we all desire the benefit of two-way relationships where both parties are willing to make equal investments for the overall enhancement of the union.

Take Away – You learn more by listening than you do by speaking. Ask yourself, am I a good listener? If you find yourself leaving a conversation knowing nothing about the person to whom you were talking, then chances are you're a bad listener.

Sheryl the Shrink, says, "Be careful of dating the same types of men by allowing them to sell you on their resumes and building up Mr. Ideal in your head. Most of the time, when we date people, we are meeting their representations or best renditions of themselves (who they can't be for an extended period of time). If you find yourself dating the same type of guys, take an assessment of yourself because the law of attraction is working. You are meeting the same type of men because you are emitting pheromones that call those boys to the yard (so to speak). Yes, darling, it's you!"

What I've Learned - Many years ago when I was single, I encountered a lot of men who fit what I thought would be my ideal mate, i.e., they were physically attractive, had great jobs, came from good families, etc. They had the package that I had built in my mind of what I thought a good mate should be AND I bought their resumes (lock, stock and barrel). If I had to grade their resumes and initial representation, they would have gotten an A+. However, when people are not being their authentic selves, it's difficult to continue the relationship for long periods of time. After the honeymoon phase (usually, 3 months), remnants of who they REALLY were began to seep out. Needless to say, who the men truly were greatly differed from the images that they were portraying, leaving me totally turned off. What I had built in my mind, in conjunction with who they were depicting, enabled me to buy into something that wasn't real. So, was it them or was it me? You guessed it, it was me!

Take Away - Pay attention to yourself and your own insecurities. What we see as our 'ideal' mate is usually unrealistic and tied to our false ideology of what we believe a 'good' man should be. Instead, use your core morals, values and gut instincts to lead you to establish authentic connections. Usually, when you connect with a person, it's organic, but this can't happen if you have a preconceived notion of how he's going to look and smell. Lose the unrealistic expectations and be open-minded. The package may not be wrapped the way you envisioned, but the contents are most of the time more than expected. That is how I ended up with my husband; I threw his resume to the wind.

Sheryl the Shrink, says, "There is often a correlation between people being emotionally and financially stingy. In other words, people who do not give freely emotionally, such as through compliments or praise, are usually as equally sparing with their money. They are withholding in every way, constipated emotionally and financially! When dating, the two often go hand-in-hand and either one can be a deal breaker."

What I've Learned – Unfortunately, I've experienced this firsthand with a guy that I dated (for a very short period).

This gentlemen, and I'm being nice, insisted that we "go Dutch" every time that we went out. Moreover, he never had a kind word to say, but he was all too forthcoming with whatever was wrong. He was easy on the eye, but hard on the heart and even harder on my wallet. In the end, it lasted longer than it should have, but it taught me more about myself than it did about him (you'll learn all about my issues as you read).

Take Away - Be a giver. You should give for the sheer satisfaction of giving. When you give emotionally and financially, you are rewarded in both prosperity and happiness.

Sheryl the Shrink, says, "Generally speaking, men fall in love with their eyes and women fall in love with their ears. Men are very visual beings who make life choices based on what they see (this may be a good reason to keep yourself up, post-marriage). In contrast, women want verbal expressiveness. We want (and need) our partners to tell us how much they love, appreciate, and cherish us. With both of these ideologies being true, how do men and women get on the same page?"

What I've Learned - The more emotionally open that men are towards women, the greater the bond that women feel in return. We lead with our hearts and will totally invest in relationships where we feel our needs can be met. This feeling of security deepens our connection and desire to be intimate with men. If men meet our emotional needs, we'll meet their physical needs, which will result in a win/win for both parties.

Take Away - Ladies, if you want to be asked out on more dates, be physically appealing and play up your assets. Men, if you want to keep a woman interested in you, get better at verbally expressing your feelings for her (and gifts on non-holidays never hurt).

Chapter 7 ~ Growth

Images available as paintings at

www.sheryltheshrink.com

Sheryl the Shrink, says, "Life is about growth and growth comes with conquering our fears. If something makes you feel uncomfortable, that is your cue to move towards it, not away from it. Nothing can parallel the confidence that comes from truly confronting and overcoming your anxieties."

What I've Learned – Fear can be stifling if you allow it to take root in your being. I had a driving phobia for many years. For whatever reason, I was deathly afraid of getting behind the wheel of a car. Whenever I needed to go somewhere, I was always dependent on someone else. It wasn't until I finished graduate school and got my first full-time job, that I was forced to confront my fear of driving.

The image of getting behind such a powerful machine paralyzed me. When I thought of driving, scenes of me hitting an unsuspecting pedestrian, running over someone in a wheelchair or mowing down a delivery man, would not leave my mind. I didn't know what to do, but I knew that I had to do something or be forever stuck in the hell-hole of public transportation.

Finally, I believed it was time to face my demons. However, I knew that before I could get behind the wheel, I had to change my mindset. Part of my fear was exaggerated by the negative images I had in my brain. When I changed my mind's movie, I changed the last scene – which was me safely operating a car. Before I knew it, I was on the road. I drove. I survived. I overcame.

Take Away – Confront your fears. Most of the time, we have built in our heads the worst case scenario, which is never as bad as we've made it. Stop missing out on opportunities to diversify your experiences. It is from these experiences that we build confidence and relinquish the power of fear that keep us stagnant in our lives.

Sheryl the Shrink, says, "Pain motivates! When people are in enough pain, they make changes. If people are not at their wit's end in their current situation, then the status quo remains. Although the status quo may not be great, it is the devil that individuals know. Therefore, there is no motivation to change their patterns."

What I've Learned – Until individuals are absolutely fed up, they are stuck in whatever ails them. Although the pain's source may be evident, many times, people retreat at the thought of addressing the feelings associated with the pain. For some, this process goes on for a lifetime, or generations, laying the groundwork for broken relationships, families, and communities.

I know this feeling all too well. For five years, I had a weight problem due to severe hypothyroidism. Although my weight was an issue, it wasn't one that I considered to be a high priority. However, I knew that I needed to lose the pounds as my 25th high school reunion approached because there was no way that I was going to be the class fat ass!

When I first decided to address my weight, I didn't know where to begin. I was skeptical of trying a nutritional cleansing program to shed the pounds, but I got to the point where the pain of being fat far outweighed (no pun intended) the fear of the unknown outcome with the program. Nevertheless, I was ready! I started the nutritional cleansing program and within four months, I'd lost 41 pounds and have kept it off for over a year.

Take Away – Allow your pain to motivate you to do better. Use your experiences to make you a better person, as well as, inspire others. Sometimes God allows us to go through certain events for the purpose of sharing our process with the world. It's helpful to understand your strife as something that you must endure for the betterment of another person. If you look at pain through these lenses, then you'll see it as an opportunity to grow, as well as, help others.

Sheryl the Shrink, says, "Do not be afraid to grow.

Growth and maturation are life's natural cycles. We all go through different phases where we start to outgrow people, places and things. In this process, we are often forced (for our own sanity) to leave behind everyone and everything to which we've once had deep connections. This is supposed to happen because some things come into your life for a reason and a season."

What I've Learned – As women, we sabotage our own growth because we are fearful of losing people, places and things. We stay in dysfunctional relationships, dead end careers, bad marriages and apartments because we are afraid to take risks, but we can only experience growth when we go outside of our comfort zone. When we aren't afraid to leave behind our past, it opens us up for brighter futures.

Take Away – Don't self-sabotage. Learn to be okay with loving people from a distance, being unfamiliar, being the 'only one' and going against the grain. True growth happens when we are brave enough to step out on faith without knowing the outcome. The reward is new experiences with new people, in different places, which ultimately increases your quality of life.

Sheryl the Shrink, says, "You always have the choice to become either the victim or victor of your circumstances. We are often not in control of what happens to us, but we are always in control of how we respond. Breaking generational curses and negative pathologies happen when people decide not to be victims or accept the status quo."

What I've Learned - Some people are born into the worst of situations. Their response to their adversity can either drive them to aspire for more or bind them to repeat negative cycles. For the people who decide to turn their adversities into reasons to succeed, these people achieve. For the people who decide to use their adversities as excuses, these people repeat cycles of generational dysfunction. At some point in all of our lives, we must ask ourselves, "Am I going to win or whine? How can I make the best of my situation?" When you make up your mind to succeed, no matter what, you make a decision to take control of your life.

Take Away – No matter your life experiences, find a way to spin it in your favor. Your attitude and how you view challenges can either work for you or against you. Change your attitude and change your life.

Sheryl the Shrink, says, "You are only in control of your part in the process, not the product. In other words, you have very little control of what happens in the end. However, the more thought and time you devote to making your moves, the more informed and better equipped you are to anticipate the outcomes. Doing your homework gives you the winning edge. If you aren't willing to get in the trenches, why bother entering the race?"

What I've Learned – Persistence pays! The more you are persistent not to fail, the more able you become. When people are determined, they rarely take no for an answer. Instead, they come up with ways to make yes answers more likely. The ways to do this are to: (1) be sure about yourself (2) be sure about what you want and (3) make sure you are the best person to receive whatever you're going after. When you establish a goal of knowing the answers to these questions, you put yourself in a better position to control the outcome.

Take Away – Take charge! Don't passively allow life to happen to you. Raise the bar, lean in and be a change agent in the things that affect your life. You'll learn in this process and you'll be inspirational to others.

Chapter 8 ~ Purpose

Images available as paintings at

www.sheryltheshrink.com

Sheryl the Shrink, says, "If you are on a particular path, and find yourself encountering roadblocks, then maybe you aren't on the route intended for your purpose. When one is on the right direction in life, opposition is minimal and the stars align."

What I've Learned - Many years ago when I enrolled in medical school, I found myself having made the most difficult decision I'd ever chosen. While it was undoubtedly the worst years of my life, it's through that process that I found my purpose.

Medical School - I was used to getting straight A's in college, sleeping well, and still having time to socialize, but in medical school that all changed. I felt like I had been thrown into a foreign land. My nights were long and no matter how much I studied, I barely passed my classes. I was on edge mentally and physically -- no food, no rest and no play! It was all work, work and more work! The more I attended class, the more resentful I became at the process. Day after day, night after night, I'd ask myself, "What am I doing?" I was miserable! Finally, I'd had enough! After two years of increased insanity, it became painfully obvious that medical school wasn't for me.

Medical school didn't give me the burn that I needed to succeed. While I did feel challenged, I didn't feel the passion to be a psychiatrist, which is what I initially went to medical school to become. I wanted to help people, in a real way. Being a pill pusher just didn't appeal to me anymore. "What could I do that really helps people?" I thought to myself. "Social Work! Yep, that's it! Social Work," I said.

When I made the decision to switch directions and get my Master's degree in Social Work, it was almost effortless. Most of the coursework really resonated with me, I aced my classes once again, I was no longer sleep deprived and I had my social life back. Things were truly smooth sailing. As a result, I had no doubt that I was on the path of doing what I was born to do. I was finally living out my life's purpose, and it felt fantastic!

Take Away - God has a plan for all of our lives. When we are truly in the space where we need to be, things will feel right. Our inner being will let us know when we are on/ off course. As God's children, we are born with specific gifts that he's placed in us to share for the greater good of the world. For this reason, I always say, "Nothing just happens." Every experience that we have is meant to add to our greater purpose. Although you may not see it at the time, feel encouraged by the fact that your adversity has been part of your journey that has happened 'for' you, not 'to' you.

Sheryl the Shrink, says, "Rejection is a part of life. Sometimes we are prepared for what life throws at us, but most of the time, we aren't. Many people go through life with grand plans of what they're going to do, where they're going to go and with whom they will be with, but the truth is, we don't know. Adding to the unknown is the fact that when we arrive at our desired destination, it may not be what we expected."

What I've Learned - After being fired from a long-term care facility as the Director of Social Services, I was confused, upset, and angry. I was efficient, very well-liked by both the staff and residents, and generally performed my job functions exceptionally well. Therefore, I had grown accustomed to a false sense of security, thinking to myself, they would never get rid of a star employee, right? Wrong!

I was confident and perhaps a bit arrogant to think that I was indispensable. So, needless to say, when I received my pink slip that read in part, "We are sorry to inform you that due to a restructure, we are terminating your position," I was floored!

At the time, every emotion possible entered my body at once. I felt angry and betrayed, but most of all I felt rejected. For the first time in my life, I didn't feel wanted. I felt deficient as a person, like I didn't measure up. Never mind that the organization was restructuring (even if that was a bunch of crap); still, I turned the rejection inward feeling like, something was wrong with me. Have you ever felt that way?

For a long time, I kicked myself trying to figure out what I could have done to prevent the termination. Then, after a while, I began to accept the fact that I couldn't have done anything. It took me a while to get it, but I began to realize that I HAD to lose that job so that I could receive the opportunity to eventually start my own private practice. See, that's the workings of God. When he closes a door, he opens a window. The experience that I took from that position has contributed towards me being a well-seasoned psychotherapist, of which I am grateful.

Take Away – What I initially thought was the worst thing to happen in my career, turned out to be the best thing to happen for my life. I had to be fired to help prepare me for my next chapter. Now, I'm living my dream, fueled by my passion, which truly helps people. I'm doing what I love to do.

Sheryl the Shrink, says, "If you are on your purposeful path, then you should feel reassured by signs or guideposts that you encounter along the way. Use your inner spirit as a vehicle to navigate your thoughts and actions. Most of the time, this is our higher power's way of communicating with us and giving us direction as to where we need to be."

What I've Learned – Sometimes it's best to let life lead you. In my maturity, I have learned to go with the flow, listen and observe my surroundings for affirmation of God's plan for me. I usually experience some sort of odd 'coincidence', but we know nothing just happens. I'm careful to listen for repetitive cues that bring home an identical thought, idea or direction. For example, I obtained my current position on a whim. The ad that I'd originally applied to was ambiguous as to the responsibilities that the job entailed. However, when I interviewed for the position, I found that not only was it exactly what I wanted, but my mom used to work in the same building. When I learned of this "coincidence", I had no doubt that this was where I was supposed to be.

Take Away - If you are questioning whether you are on the right path in your life, pay attention to the coincidences that manifest. These are no accidents; instead, they are guideposts to steer you in the proper direction.

Sheryl the Shrink, says, "Your purpose is directly related to your passion. Your passion is driven by your heart and what gives you the greatest sense of satisfaction. You (as well as all of us), were born in order to fulfill your unique destiny. We are supposed to be different because our collective gifts solve world problems."

What I've Learned - Most people are living lives of monotony; they do the same things every day in every way. When routine takes over, individuals lose their sense of passion and zest for that which makes them feel fully alive. Unfortunately, after a prolonged period of time, this becomes habit, making it harder and nearly impossible to remember what really makes them feel content. They may have the material possessions, but overall they are empty inside.

Take Away – What makes you feel happy? What would you do for free that would do wonders for another person's life? The answers to these questions are cues that will lead you to your passion. When you unlock your passion, you'll be on the road to discovering your purpose.

Sheryl the Shrink, says, "Don't spend a lot of time 'thinking' about your passion; instead, try different things starting from two lists: what makes you feel good and what comes naturally to you. A clear path to your purpose will be discovered by you trying various directions and figuring out where you get the greatest sense of fulfillment."

What I've Learned – People are happiest when they are doing what they love to do. Finding your purpose is directly related to those activities that make you feel joyous. These things may not make money, or make sense, but they give you a sense of accomplishment. When you are seeking your purpose, you must get out of your head and get into your heart. Think about it, "What pulls at my heartstrings?" What can you do to make a difference? When you assess your purpose from that perspective, chances are, you are the best person for the job.

Take Away – Finding your purpose is a very personal thing. To those around you, you may look crazy. Your purpose might drive you to leave your corporate job and start a non-profit. Whatever it is, follow your heart and chase your dreams. If you follow this recipe, you'll end up in the place that makes you happy.

Chapter 9 ~ Gratitude

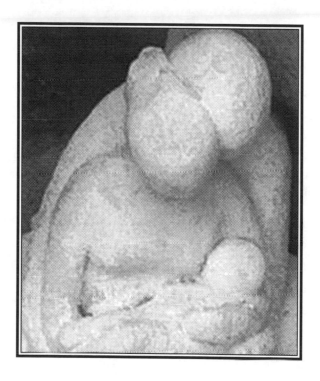

Images available as paintings at

www.sheryltheshrink.com

Sheryl the Shrink, says, "Gratitude is the key to life. No matter where we are in our lives, if we can take stock in what's going well, then the things that aren't going well are more tolerable. In order to do so, create a *'Gratitude List'* and add to it daily. In your gratitude list, focus on what you have as opposed to what you lack. For many of us, we spend too much time worrying about things that we can't change. Instead, we should put our energy into things within our control. Even if you are at a low point in your life, find at least one thing that's working in your favor."

What I've learned – When I read my gratitude list every morning and every evening, it makes me remember how truly blessed I am. There are times when I want to complain, but when I look at my gratitude list, I'm reminded that things could be worse. Staying mindful of the things that I cherish keeps me grounded and raises my level of consciousness, making me grateful for the day.

Take Away – We all have ups and downs in life. I know that sometimes the downs for some of us seem unbearable, but those are the moments when we need to be appreciative the most. Being thankful for God's daily dose of mercy and grace positions us for another day. Always be grateful for today because we don't know what tomorrow will bring.

Sheryl the Shrink, says, "We are not privy to what God has designed for us. Rather, we function with the hopes that what we envision for our lives is also what he has in store for us. As people, we generally operate by our own vices, which means, when something unplanned occurs we view it as the worst thing that could have possibly happened. In fact, the opposite is true when you are acting and living by Faith. When you are spiritually guided, then you have the understanding that a detour in your physical plan is merely an opportunity for growth and development."

What I've Learned - What exemplifies this is a problematic event that a good friend of mine recently had at his job. He had been routinely discriminated against by his supervisor. As an employee, he felt powerless. He arrived at work on time, always produced quality projects, got along well with his teammates, offered suggestions to make the organization better and volunteered to do things that other employees shunned away from. In his eyes, he was being a model employee. Therefore, he couldn't understand why he was the target of such unfair treatment. Soon, my friend began to question his worth. He stopped doing all of the things that made him such a good employee. Shortly, thereafter, he began to make excuses as to why the job he once loved was no longer a place where he belonged. He found every reason in the world to leave. Never once did my friend think to associate his treatment as a character flaw of his supervisor.

Finally, I had heard enough! I'd grown tired of my friend complaining. One day, during a heart to heart conversation, I was forced to hold my friend accountable. I told him to (pardon my French), "Grow a pair and stand up for yourself!" I helped him to see in himself what he couldn't see because the supervisor had nearly diminished his already fleeting confidence. After our conversation, he felt empowered and soon after, he was able to write a grievance that outlined his dissatisfaction with how he was being treated. Once the grievance process began, it was determined that this supervisor had treated others in the same way. The supervisor was eventually fired from his position. So, in my friend's case, what started as a negative experience, helped him to become more assertive. This was a lesson that he probably needed to learn before he could successfully transition to the next phase in his life.

Take Away – Never be afraid of a challenge. Sometimes our greatest obstacles are meant to develop some part of our character that God knows needs developing for our next chapter. When we are outside of our normal level of comfort, we pull from strength that we didn't realize that we encompassed. Always remember, you are stronger than you know.

    Sheryl the Shrink, says, "People make the world go around and gratitude in the form of being kind goes a long way. You don't meet people by chance. You never know the function that an ordinary encounter will play in your life. The universe is designed to bring people into our lives for very specific reasons. From the most casual of meets to lifelong friendships, everyone in your life is there to play a role and/or teach you a lesson. If you approach all of your interactions in this manner, it will help you to broaden your appreciation for people."

What I've Learned – As I've matured, I've learned to treasure the value of a good interaction. While not everyone will be in your life for a long period of time, it's important to qualify your interactions in ways that make a positive impact. We never know a person's struggles. Therefore, going out of your way to pay the toll for the person behind you, paying for two coffees for the next in line or complimenting someone on his/her outfit can make a person's day. When you can add meaning to a person's life, with little or no effort, as God's children, we have a responsibility to do so.

Take Away – People may not remember your name or what you said, but they will always remember how you made them feel.

Sheryl the Shrink, says, "Be of good cheer, volunteer! There's no better way to show gratitude than doing something nice for someone else. The principle of 'paying it forward' is life-changing and necessary to make the world progress. Taking the time to meet the needs of others is required work of God."

What I've Learned – People are too caught up in what's going on in their little parts of the world. We live in a society where people are starving, homeless and severely down on their luck. When we take the time to get over ourselves, we are much better prepared to be part of the solution to some of life's longstanding problems. We all have time and talent that can be used for the greater good.

Take Away – There is someone else in need of what you have to offer. Visit the nearest hospital, call the nearest shelter or go to the most impoverished area in your neighborhood and find out what you can do to help.

   Sheryl the Shrink, says, "Showing gratitude is giving up your right to complain. While we all have things in our lives which are complaint worthy, what good does it do? Instead of expressing discontent, focus on the many ways that your situation could have been worse."

What I've Learned – People who chronically complain are not only miserable, but they inevitably make those around them miserable. Chronic whiners spend too much time concentrating on the things that aren't right in their lives. They waste precious moments looking at life through pessimistic lenses. These people are determined to be unhappy and can infect the environment around them.

Take Away – In all things be grateful. "Thank you", are two of the most powerful words that can change your life from one of woe to one of bliss.

Chapter 10 ~ Spirituality

Images available as paintings at

www.sheryltheshrink.com

Sheryl the Shrink, says, "Whenever life seems completely overwhelming and you are experiencing various external stressors, remember to surrender to God. Acknowledge that a particular situation is out of your control and choose to relinquish all possible outcomes to your higher power."

What I've Learned - Everything ultimately happens for the greater good. When I was terminated from my position of Director of Social Services, I could have easily obtained other equivalent jobs in that field. This would have been the safe thing to do because my experience at the time was limited. However, I made a radical choice to go out on Faith, by applying for jobs where I was barely qualified. Through a person's eyes, it seemed impossible that I would obtain such a position, but with God, I knew it was achievable. I believed, I trusted and he came through, as he always will.

Take Away – In your greatest times of need are when you should trust that God will take care of you. I know sometimes that horrendous predicaments make it extremely challenging to see the good in life, however, this happens to all of us. I understand how it may seem as if your situation is beyond a solution, but believe me, it's not. God can do all things if you trust in him and allow him to work on your behalf.

Sheryl the Shrink, says, "We are all God's children and the Holy Spirit lives within us. We are all uniquely created with special gifts that are supposed to make the world a better place. While we each experience life differently, in God's eyes, we are all equal. When we approach life knowing that his love endures forever, then we are free to experience life fully present in the form of our best selves."

What I've Learned – When you're in touch with your spirit you have a greater appreciation for the simple things in life. You ground yourself in the very essence of being alive and suddenly nothing else matters. This is how I feel whenever I'm around animals or out in nature. I feel totally surrendered to my being that breathes life into me. Today, I'm happy to say, "I'm grateful for the little things."

Take Away – Take the time to feel your spirit within. Use techniques such as meditation, yoga, nature and quiet time to be with yourself. When we silence the distractions in our lives, we clear our heart space to absorb the things that really matter.

Sheryl the Shrink, says, "The universe has a way of continuously putting you in similar situations until you learn the desired lesson. Each time we miss the mark, our intended target becomes a little harder to achieve."

What I've Learned – We allow ourselves to get in our own way because as humans we want what we want. However, many times our plans aren't consistent with those that God has intended for us. For this reason, we make the same mistakes over and over again. We end up at the same points because we keep trying to take the same route to get to a different place. If it's something that we really want, we try every rational (and irrational) way to make the ending our desired outcome. For some of us, it takes years to finally realize that what we're seeking isn't for us.

Take Away – Stop being stubborn. You don't always have to learn from your own errors. Rather, you can learn from the mistakes of others. Sometimes it shouldn't take a brick to fall on your head before you get the message. What's meant for you will be yours, but if it's not meant for you, don't waste valuable time trying to achieve it.

Sheryl the Shrink, says, "Karma is real. You definitely reap what you sow, so always make a conscious effort to treat others well, and do the right thing, no matter how difficult it may be."

What I've Learned – The universe has a way of bringing life full circle. The energy that you put out definitely makes itself back to you at some point. When we do well for others because it's the noble thing to do, the universe will do right by us. It takes a special person to see others in a good light no matter how they treat you. Difficult people are sometimes placed in our lives as tests to see if we still hold God's principles of love. If we pass, many times, we are rewarded, but if we fail, more and more of those people enter our lives. The goal is to kill them with kindness in hopes that your kindness will rub off.

Take Away – What goes around comes back again. Make sure when it comes your way that it doesn't bite you in the butt!

Sheryl the Shrink, says, "Believing in a higher power means having another source of strength and energy. It's impossible to think that as human beings we can solely manage the complexities of existing all by ourselves. When you trust a force greater than yourself, then you have someone to carry you when the road of life becomes too much to bear."

What I've Learned – As I've developed as a person, I've also grown in my faith. When I think about my life and the various ways that it could have played out, I'm instantly grateful. One of the greatest lessons that I've learned in my journey is that it's not all about me. Life is about helping other people and being a Sheppard to lead other people to places of fulfillment. When you reach a point where you can truly appreciate the blessings that God has given you, then it's difficult to be selfish. This is something that I've had to learn, and when I did, it made me a better human being.

Today, I'm in tune with my higher power and my purpose for being on this earth. Each day that I awake, I'm thankful to be alive. When you think about the alternative, you should be instantly joyous that he chose you to see another day.

Take Away – There is no greater love than the love of God.

Crisis Chapter ~ Why Me? Why Now?

This chapter is dedicated to those experiencing an extreme crisis. I understand that at various times in our lives, we all feel paralyzed by life's nuances. Being people, sometimes we plan our lives in a way that doesn't account for alternate courses of action. Therefore, when those unplanned things occur, we feel overwhelmed, defeated and desperate for help.

Listen, first of all, I hear you. You may feel on the brink of an emotional breakdown and/or may even be contemplating suicide, but I need you to understand that **your life absolutely matters**. While I know it's a difficult concept to grasp when it seems as if everything is falling apart around you, but, you are uniquely designed to handle the challenges that you're experiencing.

God has prepared each of us with the tools necessary to thrive in our lives. Some of us are 'built to bear', which means that we are gifted with the strength to shoulder burdens that would break most. So, if you are a person who finds yourself with your fair share of obstacles, then consider yourself chosen by God. Think about it this way, God thought that you were the best fit for your life. He has given you what you need to make a positive impact in this world; otherwise, you would not have been born. Since we all are operators in a larger plan, God's Will would not be fulfilled without your contributions. Therefore, be fully reassured that the world needs YOU!

With that being said, "Trust me, I get it." All of this is much easier spoken than done when you're in active crisis. I understand that it can be hard to see the light at the end of the tunnel when you're buried with your eyes shut. However, that's when Faith should take over your thought process. If you can think about your life as purposeful, then you understand that your crisis is especially designed for your emotional and spiritual growth. What you are going through is happening for a constructive reason and it will bring forth your inner fortitude.

One of the hardest things to remember when you're in crisis is that your circumstances are temporary. Many times, during this phase in your life, the magnitude of the situation can seem like an eternity. As otherwise multi-functioning adults, when you are blindsided by crisis, there are still other people who are depending on you. The responsibility and pressure to be emotionally present for others often extends your personal crisis. During this time, your ability to process your own stuff becomes stifled, thus, dragging on the duration of the problem. However, nothing lasts forever.

Listen, I'm a therapist, but before I'm a therapist, I'm a woman and I've had my share of life's challenges. There was a point in my life when I was consumed by internal and external circumstances that I couldn't control. At that time, I didn't know how to access the tools that I needed to help myself. As a therapist, I felt useless. I was inundated by my own insecurities that told me that I wasn't good enough. Even though I'd helped hundreds of families through crisis, still, when I needed me most, I couldn't show up in my own life. It's one thing to be a lay person and not have the tools, but it's consciously scary to be a therapist unable to unleash your own emotional freedom.

When I was experiencing my low, I thought my life was over. I can remember this time being extremely dark. No matter what I did, I couldn't find happiness anywhere in my existence. I was emotionally drained. Then, one day, I was simply tired of being tired. I'd grown exhausted of feeling sorry for myself so I decided, enough was enough. Instead of dwelling on the negatives, I started putting all of my energy into the positives. Soon, my days started looking brighter and my breakthrough presented itself. Through the power of prayer and counseling, I found myself again.

Even though I was at the lowest period in my life, I am grateful for it because it humbled me. I believe that experience has made me a better person and psychotherapist. I know what I'm made of now and I am stronger than I have ever been. You see, with God, there's always hope.

Remember to be the hero in your own life; be the victor and not the victim. If you believe that you can, you will overcome your struggles. I know sometimes we can't see or access our own strength, so recognize when to ask for help. I thank God for counseling, because not only has it helped me, but it has enabled me to help others. If you need a higher level of care than a counselor can provide, then go to your nearest hospital's emergency room. There, you will be properly evaluated to receive the most appropriate services for your level of assistance. Even if you require inpatient treatment at a residential facility, that's okay too, go and get what you need. The bottom line is, your life is worth it and so are you!

Last, but not least, remember to take each day one day at a time, each hour one hour at a time, each minute one minute at a time, and each second one second at a time. This way, whatever you are facing feels more manageable. If you ever feel all alone and/or unloved, know that you're never alone. God is always with you.

Resource Chapter ~ National Hotline Numbers

Whether you're in crisis or are just looking for help for a friend or family member, there are dozens of organizations available to help you deal with a variety of immediate concerns, from crisis situations and domestic violence, to rape and substance abuse. Most of these hotlines are available 24 hours a day, and can help you with whatever level of assistance you need — from general information about the subject, to helping you find an immediate intervention. The hotlines below are listed in alphabetical order according to topic.

If you're suicidal, I recommend contacting the **National Suicide Prevention Lifeline toll-free at 800-273-8255**. Additional crisis and suicide hotlines are available in the category below, Crises and Suicide.

Sheryl Schembari, LCSW

AIDS

AIDS Hotline
(800) FOR-AIDS

American Social Health Association: Sexually
Transmitted Disease Hotline
(800) 227-8922

CDC AIDS Information
(800) 232-4636

AIDS Info: Treatment, Prevention and Research
(800) HIV-0440

National AIDS Hotline
(800) 342-AIDS

ALCOHOL

Alcohol Hotline
(800) 331-2900

Al-Anon for Families of Alcoholics
(800) 344-2666

Alcohol and Drug Helpline
(800) 821-4357

Alcohol Treatment Referral Hotline
(800) 252-6465

Alcohol & Drug Abuse Hotline
(800) 729-6686

Families Anonymous
(800) 736-9805

National Council on Alcoholism and Drug Dependence
Hopeline
(800) 622-2255

CHILD ABUSE

Child Protection Hotline (Los Angeles County DCFS)
Within CA (800) 540-4000
Outside CA (213) 283-1960

Judge Baker Children's Center – Child Abuse Hotline
(800) 792-5200

Child Help USA National Child Abuse Hotline
(800) 422-4453

Covenant House
(800) 999-9999

National US Child Abuse Hotline
(800) 422-4453

CRISES AND SUICIDE

Girls & Boys Town National Hotline
(800) 448-3000

International Suicide Hotlines

National Hopeline Network
(800) SUICIDE

National Suicide Prevention Lifeline
(800) 273-TALK (8255)

National Youth Crisis Hotline
(800) 442-HOPE (4673)

DOMESTIC VIOLENCE

National Domestic Violence Hotline
(800) 799-7233

MEDICAL

American Association of Poison Control Centers
(800) 222-1222

American Social Health: STD Hotline
(800) 227-8922

OTHER

Shoplifters Anonymous
(800) 848-9595

Eating Disorders Awareness and Prevention
(800) 931-2237

San Francisco Sex Information
(415) 989-SFSI

Teen Help Adolescent Resources
(800) 840-5704

PREGNANCY

Planned Parenthood Hotline
(800) 230-PLAN (230-7526)

RAPE AND SEXUAL ASSAULT

Rape, Abuse, and Incest National Network (RAINN)
(800) 656-HOPE

National Domestic Violence/Child Abuse/Sexual Abuse
(800) 799-7233

Abuse Victim Hotline
(866) 662-4535

RUNNING AWAY

National Runaway Switchboard
(800) 231-6946

National Hotline for Missing & Exploited Children
(800) 843-5678

Child Find of America
(800) 426-5678

SUBSTANCE ABUSE

National Institute on Drug Abuse Hotline
(800) 662-4357

Cocaine Anonymous
(800) 347-8998

National Help Line for Substance Abuse
(800) 262-2463

Source: The Center for Mental Health in Schools

Acknowledgments

Throughout the past fourteen years, my husband, Marco, has constantly encouraged me to chase my dream of becoming a writer. He has never faltered in his belief in me, and has always supported my pursuit to achieve my goals.

My parents have forever been by my side. They have raised me to be confident, self-sufficient and competent. No matter how big my dreams or grand my plans, they gave me the courage to reach for the stars.

My mother and father-in-law, Marcella and Sal, have graciously welcomed me into their family and supported me in every way imaginable. They have never missed an opportunity to give of themselves and for that, I am eternally grateful.

My terrific group of girlfriends, especially Krista Deckhut, Elaine Lew, Cindy Underwood, Beth Rosenthal,

Lauren Horvath, Jennifer Carbone, Kim Armenti, Amy Wilensky, Kimberly Volpe, Laura Steinberg, Azra Defoe, Saadia Rehman and Ruby Gonzalez, thank you for always having my back.

To my Facebook family, thank you for listening and helping me to understand that my words made a difference. It is through you that this idea came about. You have been my original audience starting with my Sheryl the Shrink, says, blogs. It is from that forum that this concept came to life.

Last, but not least, I acknowledge my editor, LaTia McNeely-Sandiford, MSW, founder of Lions Vision Productions and Sister Social Worker, who gets it! Through this process, she has been beyond impressive with her time management skills, creativity and expert feedback. Through her knowledge and vision, my blogs became my book. Thank you for helping me to live my dream.